Teach a *45 Days With* Workshop or Course

Would you like to use one of our *45 Days With* books to teach a class or to create a 7 week series at your church, school or other organization? It's an easy and powerful way to support your community and generate revenue.

All *45 Days With* books are actually 49 days, as we provide 4 bonus days with each book for a complete 7 week course.

Most teachers charge $30-50 per course participant and meet weekly to discuss the week of journaling with participants.

Church Ministers use the books to lead their organization through a 7 week series at their Sunday Service. It actually causes the congregation to do weekly journaling homework.

Visit **www.avaiya.com/45dayswithcourse** to purchase *45 Days With* books at up to 75% off for your class or organization.

45 Days with

A COURSE IN MIRACLES

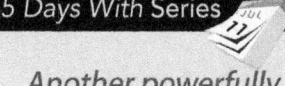

The 45 Days With Series

Another powerfully uplifting book from AVAIYA founders, iKE ALLEN & Ande Anderson, MS, RD.

Discover their books, courses and possibly yourself at www.AVAIYA.com

iKE ALLEN & ANDE ANDERSON, MS, RD

AVAIYA edition 2014
Copyright © 2014 by iKE ALLEN

All rights reserved. This book, or parts thereof, may not be reproduced in any form without permission, except in the case of brief quotations embodied in critical articles and reviews.

A paperback original

Cover & Book design by iKE ALLEN

Book layout by Ande Anderson, MS, RD

Printed in the United States of America

10 9 8 7 6 5 4 3 2 1

AVAIYA
A Limited Liability Company
6397 Glenmoor Road
Boulder, CO 80303
www.AVAIYA.com

CONTENTS

INTRODUCTION..7

WEEK 1: KENNETH WAPNICK...12

WEEK 2: LYN CORONA...26

WEEK 3: GARY RENARD..40

WEEK 4: JON MUNDY...54

WEEK 5: NOUK SANCHEZ..68

WEEK 6: LINDA CARPENTER..82

WEEK 7: KENNETH WAPNICK...96

Bonus Days...102

ABOUT THE AUTHORS..111

INTRODUCTION

This powerfully loving *45 Days With* book is designed to accelerate your awakening by simplifying the often challenging task of reading the entire public domain book, *A Course in Miracles*. In this wonderfully small book, we combine the modern day wisdom and knowledge of several contemporary teachers of *A Course in Miracles*, such as Ken Wapnick, Gary Renard, Nouk Sanchez, and Jon Mundy with a transformative journaling action step each day.

One of the most amazing parts of the book, *A Course in Miracles*, is that it specifically states that "a universal theology is impossible, but a universal experience is not only possible but necessary." It emphasizes that it is but one version of the universal curriculum. There are many others, this one differing from them only in form. They all lead to God in the end.

As most spiritual practices promote that their model has the truth, it has been refreshing to explore *A Course in Miracles* knowing that it clearly states it is only one of many versions of the universal curriculum. Ken Wapnick and other teachers have studied a plethora of different paths throughout

Teach a class with a *45 Days With* book. Learn how at
www.avaiya.com/45dayswithcourse

their lives and we believe this is part of what allows them to be so relatable to everyone they encounter.

The teachers and *A Course in Miracles* are highlighted for a moment of each day, and then you have the opportunity to accelerate your own spiritual journey, by journaling and/or practicing scribing in the accompanying pages.

All the wisdom and insights shared within these pages from the teachers, are from my interviews, talks and phone conversations with them during the years we have known them. I hope you find this material beneficial in your journey, as Ken Wapnick says, "to the other side of the bridge."

You can additionally see Ken and other *ACIM* teachers featured in our books, films and more, available at http://www.avaiya.com/ACIM.

To fully benefit from this version of *45 Days with A Course in Miracles*, please journal each day. It is not a task, but a wonderful opportunity to truly learn more about yourself and *ACIM*. If you miss a day, simply pick up where you left off last.

Digital Ebook Readers: If you're reading a digital version of this book, it may allow you to type directly into the document. If not, many ereaders like iPads, Android Tablets, Kindle Fire, etc., provide access to apps that you can journal in. Please search your app store or search to find one that works for you.

You can also go to www.45DaysWith.com to share your experiences and read about others on their *45 Days With* journey.

We hope you find joy, Inspiration and wisdom from this philosophy and your journaling.

Teach a class with a *45 Days With* book. Learn how at
www.avaiya.com/45dayswithcourse

Visit the 45 Days With community and share your journey:
www.45DaysWith.com

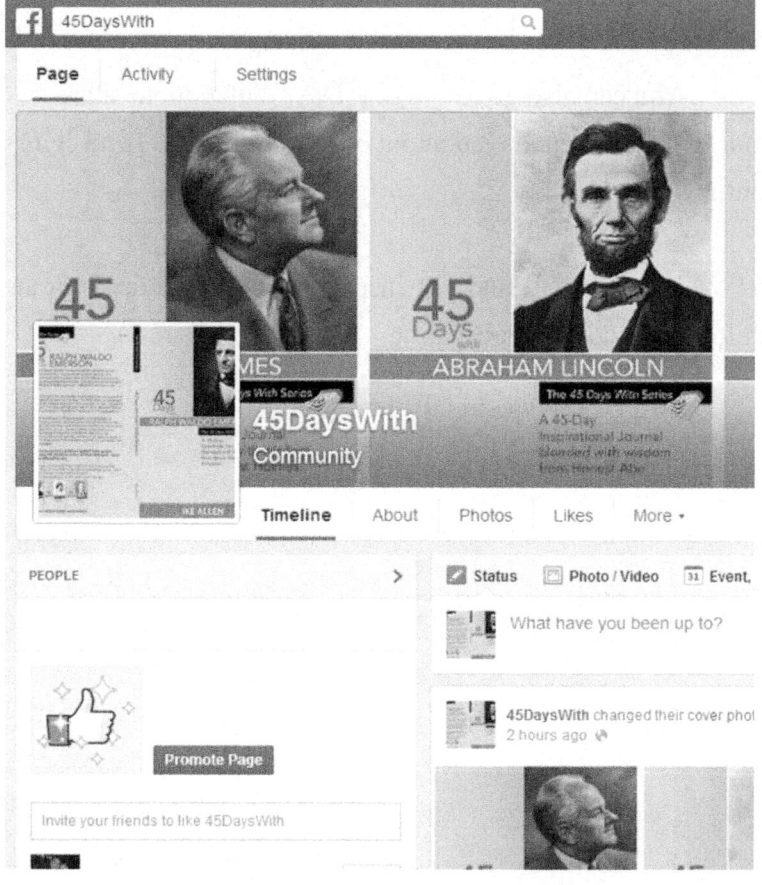

45 Days with *A Course in Miracles*

This extraordinary book belongs to:

_____

You are about to co-author your own book with *A Course in Miracles*, iKE ALLEN & Ande Anderson, by journaling in these pages.

Invite your friends to do this book with you! Email, Facebook, or call them, and you can all begin your journey together.

Please list the three things you would most like to experience during your next 45 Days with *A Course in Miracles*. (It could be as simple as choosing three of these: Awakening, Joy, Peace, Love, Inspiration, Gratitude, Integrity, Prosperity, Freedom, Forgiveness, Health, Appreciation, Enlightenment).

To fully benefit from this book, please list three now before turning the page:

1. _____

2. _____

3. _____

Teach a class with a *45 Days With* book. Learn how at
www.avaiya.com/45dayswithcourse

WEEK 1
Kenneth Wapnick

Forgiveness in The Course *is different from how it is usually thought of. Typically, when we think of forgiveness, we think someone has done something to us or to those people with whom we identify. That requires us to forgive them their sin.* The Course's *position on forgiveness is that we forgive them for what they have not done, not for what they have done. Metaphysically of course, what this means is, since there is no world then there is nothing to forgive. But on a practical level, which is really the most important part of this course - if you can't live this and demonstrate it, then it doesn't mean anything - on this level, what it means is that what I forgive you for, is that you have not taken God's love away from me. ~* **Kenneth Wapnick**

45 Days with *A Course in Miracles*

"Those you do not forgive you fear."
-*A Course in Miracles*

Day 1: Do you believe on the practical level that anyone here has taken God's love away from you? Think hard of everyone you've ever interacted with - ex spouses, ex lovers, ex friends, etc. Can you do something today to live and demonstrate forgiveness? For me, my divorce was one of my greatest opportunities to practice forgiveness. Afterwards, journal about what happened. -iKE

_____
_____
_____
_____
_____
_____
_____
_____
_____
_____
_____
_____

Teach a class with a *45 Days With* book. Learn how at www.avaiya.com/45dayswithcourse

The key element in all unforgiveness is that you have done something so reprehensible, so unconscionable, that nothing in the universe could ever bring me to forgive you because of what you've done. Whether you've done it on a national scale, an international scale or whether you've done it in my personal life. And all that I'm really doing is retaining a very shabby image of myself that says, "I am this worthless, vulnerable, helpless person. A victim of forces and powers and people beyond my control who can do with me what they will, and have the power to take my happiness away from me."
~ **Kenneth Wapnick**

45 Days with *A Course in Miracles*

"Forgiveness, salvation, Atonement, true perception, all are one." -*A Course in Miracles*

Day 2: Do you still believe today that there are people that have done something so reprehensible, so unconscionable, that nothing in the universe could ever bring you to forgive them? It is very important to be honest about "what is." If you chose the teacher of happiness, would you be happy? Share in your journal. -**Ande**

_____

_____

_____

_____

_____

_____

_____

_____

_____

_____

_____

Teach a class with a *45 Days With* book. Learn how at
www.avaiya.com/45dayswithcourse

No one can take my happiness away from me except myself. Because happiness is not found in the world. It's not found in my body getting it's needs met. Happiness is found in choosing the teacher of happiness, which could be the Holy Spirit or Jesus, that teach that sin and guilt are not real and that nothing has happened. Not one note in Heaven's song is missed, The Course *says. That nothing happened to interfere with the perfect love and the perfect oneness of Heaven. Creator and Created. Cause and effect. Source and the effect of that source have never been separated. Therefore there is nothing to forgive.* ~ **Kenneth Wapnick**

"Only in someone else can you forgive yourself...."
-A Course in Miracles

Day 3: Imagine being constantly aware that you never separated and yet, you're still having this experience on this planet called earth. How would your life look and feel without guilt and shame? Put pen to paper and paint a picture of your life when filled with love. -iKE

_____

_____

_____

_____

_____

_____

_____

_____

_____

_____

Teach a class with a *45 Days With* book. Learn how at
www.avaiya.com/45dayswithcourse

*We all accuse ourselves of having committed the unpardonable sin of separating from our source. That's what we believe. And we built this whole world to protect us from the disastrous consequences of God's wrath in our minds because that's where the sin occurred. So we make up a world of bodies and seek to hide there - a world of mindlessness. And, of course, what this does is fulfill the Ego's strategy that "If I don't know if I have a mind, how can I change my mind and choose the Holy Spirit as my teacher?" The Ego makes up a world and makes up a separate body into which we think we are born. And that makes us mindless. ~***Kenneth Wapnick***

"Freedom from illusions lies only in not believing them."
- A Course in Miracles

Day 4: If you truly wish to awaken, you must forgive yourself for something you did not do, and on the practical level, you must forgive anyone you have projected guilt onto. Do you really want to awaken? Have you truly forgiven yourself and everyone in your life? Your parents? Old friends? Co-workers? -iKE

Teach a class with a *45 Days With* book. Learn how at www.avaiya.com/45dayswithcourse

I can't change a mind I don't know I have. So what I then do, is I take this sin I believe I've committed, I project it out onto other people and blame them. But what has to be forgiven is not what I believe the world has done to me. What has to be forgiven is what I believe I did to the world. I chose to make other people sinful and guilty and responsible for my own secret sin - that I'm the one who separated from God's love. And so I forgive you for what you've not done. Because regardless of what you may have done with your body to my body, you have not had any effect on my mind. So forgiveness then means simply, that I return to my mind. I recall the projections of my guilt I put onto you, I bring the guilt back within and I recognize that guilt is something that I made. Not only did I make up my anger at you, but, I made up my own guilt. ~ **Kenneth Wapnick**

"That there is choice is an illusion." *-A Course in Miracles*

Day 5: Today, bring the guilt you've projected onto others back to your own mind. Journal about it in your own mind and share your thoughts on choosing against it in your journal -**iKE**

Teach a class with a *45 Days With* book. Learn how at www.avaiya.com/45dayswithcourse

The Holy Spirit is the great principle that nothing happened. It's what The Course *calls the principle of Atonement. Nothing happened. There was no separation. And if nothing happened, there was no sin. And if I did not sin, there's nothing to project. So when I forgive, I basically am reporting what* The Course *calls "The Three Steps of Forgiveness." It isn't called that but it enumerates these three steps. The first step says, you're not the source of my problem. Because the guilt is not in you, it's in me. Again, regardless of what you've done, your Ego is not my problem. I breathe the guilt that I've projected onto you back onto my own mind. And the second step, I look at the guilt in my mind and realize I've chosen it. And because I've chosen it, I can choose against it. And, that's it. I'm done.*
~ **Kenneth Wapnick**

45 Days with *A Course in Miracles*

"The dreamer of a dream is not awake, but does not know he sleeps." -*A Course in Miracles*

Day 6: In our interactive video presentation, *Unity in A Course in Miracles,* we often ask participants, "What better choice could you make today if you brought a perceived problem from the dream, back to the mind?" Share or scribe your answer to this in your journal today. **-iKE & Ande**

_____

_____

_____

_____

_____

_____

_____

_____

_____

_____

_____

_____

Teach a class with a *45 Days With* book. Learn how at www.avaiya.com/45dayswithcourse

When I change my mind about it, it disappears. By realizing that I chose the wrong teacher and I see the disastrous consequences of that mistaken choice, I'm automatically going to choose the correct one. There's a line in the text that says, "Who with the love of God upholding him would find a choice between miracles and murder hard to make?" Who with the love of God upholding him, which occurs when we become right minded, would find a choice between miracles and murder hard to make? All forgiveness does, the miracle does, (which is why the book is called A Course in Miracles) *is bring the problem from the dream, from the world and body, back to the mind so I can realize I made a mistaken choice. I can make a better one and that's it. I'll automatically choose the right teacher, a teacher that will lead me to this quiet joy, this peace that just permeates everything, that embraces everyone without exception. That's how forgiveness works. ~* **Kenneth Wapnick**

"**There is a place in you where there is perfect peace.**"
                                                        -*A Course in Miracles*

Day 7: Today, take an honest look at whether you are participating in this process to authentic Peace of Mind, or if you are doing it to change something in your outside world. Share authentically. -iKE

_____
_____
_____
_____
_____
_____
_____
_____
_____
_____
_____
_____
_____
_____

Teach a class with a *45 Days With* book. Learn how at
www.avaiya.com/45dayswithcourse

WEEK 2
Lyn Corona

In A Course in Miracles, *forgiveness is our way home. It's the withdrawal of our belief in the false. First of all, our education in* The Course *in the beginning teaches us the difference between the true and the false. It tells us that our Ego thinking - our thoughts of separation, our thoughts of attack, our thoughts of defense, our need to protect - all of those mechanisms of the Ego - the false sense of self, the false sense of identity, the sense of false authorship (as if I authored myself) - all of those illusions must be undone.* ~ **Lyn Corona**

45 Days with *A Course in Miracles*

"It is your thoughts alone that cause you pain."
-A Course in Miracles

Day 8: Have you ever had the experience of blending into oneness with another person? You have been one *and* you experience duality. In our workshops, we often do an exercise called, BE WITH, that allows people to see themselves in others. Do you believe you can return to Unity Consciousness *and* experience duality? Share your thoughts in your journal today. -**Ande**

Teach a class with a *45 Days With* book. Learn how at www.avaiya.com/45dayswithcourse

The Course *teaches us that the false sense of authorship I made for myself - here I am as a separated, long lasting individual entity and that I'm in charge here - is filled with an enormous sense of guilt that we're not even aware of. That I have my own will. And, that I have my own needs and wants and desires. And, the need to have those fulfilled. That idea that I exist as a separated self - in order to have done that in* The Course's *metaphysics - I have to have imagined that I annihilated the oneness of Heaven. That I, in a sense committed a celestial homicide and that I killed God and now He's out to get me. I'm guilty and he's out to get me. And we're not aware on a conscious level of the enormous guilt that the false sense of authorship that self-identity causes.* ~ **Lyn Corona**

"The truth is simple; it is one without an opposite."
-A Course in Miracles

Day 9: How could the One become many? We know what *The Course* says, but what thoughts or Inspirations come from inside *you* when you put pen to paper today? -i**KE**

_____

_____

_____

_____

_____

_____

_____

_____

_____

_____

_____

_____

Teach a class with a *45 Days With* book. Learn how at
www.avaiya.com/45dayswithcourse

What we do in order to try to maintain some sense of peace, is we project that guilt. We can't project what we are. We can only project what we're not. We project it out onto others. All of our upsets with others and what they're showing us are really an opportunity to look at the guilt that we projected outside of ourselves. In other words, the purpose that the Ego has for all of our relationships is to use them as a screen upon which to project our pain and misery and suffering - our guilt, in other words - and, say, "You're the cause of my pain. It isn't my false sense of authorship. It isn't that I separated, and believe that I've accomplished this. That's not the problem." So, I get to keep my false sense of identity, and I get to blame somebody else for it and say, "You're the cause of it."
~ **Lyn Corona**

> "**What you think you are is a belief to be undone.**"
> *-A Course in Miracles*

Day 10: Was Buddha Enlightened? Did he experience being in this world but not of this world? *The Course* says, "a universal theology is impossible, but a universal experience is not only possible but necessary." I remember Ken Wapnick telling me that most *ACIM* students forget the part of *The Course* that says, "It emphasizes application rather than theory, and experience rather than theology." Are you applying the principle of *The Course* in your life, or are you a person that simply talks about what *The Course* says? Today, journal about what my question brings up for you. Allow yourself to authentically share your feelings in your journal.
-iKE

Teach a class with a *45 Days With* book. Learn how at
www.avaiya.com/45dayswithcourse

Forgiveness is simply seeing that whoever it is out there that I'm blaming at the moment for my misery, that what I think you're doing to me has really not occurred. ~ **Lyn Corona**

"**Love is one. It has no separate parts and no degrees.**"
-*A Course in Miracles*

Day 11: Again today, we're going to challenge you in regard to theology and specifically, *ACIM* theology. Are you able today to seek only the experience? If I tell you I am enlightened, what does this bring up for you? Are you able to remember perfect Oneness? Do you want to challenge my statement? What does *The Course* tell you to do? Share in your journal today. -iKE

_____
_____
_____
_____
_____
_____
_____
_____
_____
_____

Teach a class with a *45 Days With* book. Learn how at www.avaiya.com/45dayswithcourse

Forgiveness ultimately becomes a state of mind in which we are able to look at the insanity, the chaos, the confusion, the suffering, the pain that we see outside. To look at that with no judgment - that's forgiveness. Forgiveness is still. It's quiet. It judges not. It looks. It watches. It waits. And, it does nothing.
~ **Lyn Corona**

"Jesus became what all of you must be."
-A Course in Miracles

Day 12: Mahatma Gandhi said, "Whatever you do will be insignificant, but it is very important that you do it." This is clearly another paradox that makes sense when we do not think, but *feel*. What do you feel today? Do you feel Holy Spirit wanting to speak through you in your journal today? As I write this, I *feel* my connection to you, I *feel* our Oneness. Share your feelings. **-Ande**

_____

_____

_____

_____

_____

_____

_____

_____

_____

_____

_____

_____

Teach a class with a *45 Days With* book. Learn how at www.avaiya.com/45dayswithcourse

To do something is to say, "that's real." So what we learn to do is to look at it with that affection, with that awareness, with that presence of love, so the looking in The Course *is you looking with the Holy Spirit. Or you looking with your teacher. But a symbol of love where you look gently with soft eyes and you don't try to fix or change what isn't real. What's real doesn't need fixing and what's not real can't be fixed. It's really that simple. Bring that presence to everything. Let the illusion wind down, by not reacting, not responding.*

~ **Lyn Corona**

"Perception is a choice and not a fact."
-*A Course in Miracles*

Day 13: Are you peaceful today? In reading Lyn's passage, do you see how you could be peaceful always? Today, allow Holy Spirit to guide you in your journaling and share what peace feels like for you. For me, peace feels like all the weight of worry, judgment, and hate being lifted off me, followed by an embrace in the delicate arms of love. -**Ande**

Teach a class with a *45 Days With* book. Learn how at www.avaiya.com/45dayswithcourse

This is forgiveness in A Course in Miracles. *It's not forgiving you because of something you did. It's seeing that it never happened in the first place. It was all just projected. And all just imagined.*

~ **Lyn Corona**

"Do not see error. Do not make it real."
-A Course in Miracles

Day 14: Plato said, "I am the wisest man alive, for I know one thing, and that is that I know nothing." What do you believe you know? Do you believe that as you get older you know more than people younger than you? When you return to Right Mind, what happens? Do you laugh? Cry? Rest? Can you see you're always safe at home? **-iKE**

_____

_____

_____

_____

_____

_____

_____

_____

_____

_____

Teach a class with a *45 Days With* book. Learn how at www.avaiya.com/45dayswithcourse

WEEK 3
Gary Renard

There's a place in A Course in Miracles *called The Self Accused. It may look like we're judging and condemning other people. But the truth is, we have accused ourselves first. And then we choose to see it in other people and project it on to other people. It looks like we're accusing them. The truth is, we actually accused ourselves first. But when that becomes denied and unconscious, it's projected. Psychologists will tell you that projection always follows denial because it has to go somewhere. And then you choose to see it in others.* ~ **Gary Renard**

"All are called but few choose to listen."
-*A Course in Miracles*

Day 15: The body is in the mind. You are safely at home and you're still having the experience of this life. If someone needs help, what is the loving thing to do? I often ask myself this question, especially when I'm having the experience of someone pushing my buttons. Who could you help today that you would normally judge or blame for the situation they need help with? -**Ande**

The Course *teaches us that the thinking of the world must be reversed. What we need to do is undo that projection. Reverse it. The way out of illusions, the way out of nightmares, the way out of the dream is to reverse it. That's how the Ego gets undone. Because as you forgive those things that you see in other people, that are right there in front of you, the truth is, you're the one who's being forgiven. It just doesn't look that way at first. The cool part is that as you do it, you actually start to experience that you're being forgiven. You actually start to experience your own innocence.*
~ **Gary Renard**

"All your time is spent in dreaming."
-A Course in Miracles

Day 16: Buddha said, "The mind is everything. What you think you become." Today, think and journal about your innocence. Imagine you are forgiven eternally. **-Ande**

Teach a class with a *45 Days With* book. Learn how at www.avaiya.com/45dayswithcourse

A Course in Miracles *is a spiritual experience. Most people think that it's an intellectual exercise. But the world doesn't need another intellectual exercise.*

*~ **Gary Renard***

***"You* are the dreamer of the world of dreams."**
-A Course in Miracles

Day 17: When you let go of the idea that you're actually here, the awareness that you're safely at home returns. Are you ready to hold onto this awareness as you walk within the dream? Today, put pen to paper and simply let Holy Spirit guide you. Perhaps, you'll write nothing. Perhaps, you'll draw a picture? **-Ande**

Teach a class with a *45 Days With* book. Learn how at www.avaiya.com/45dayswithcourse

At one point, The Course *says, "This is not a course in theosophical speculation. It is only concerned with forgiveness or the correctness of perception." What it's really talking about is changing your perception, looking at the world differently and undoing the Ego. According to* The Course, *that is a fast way to get home.* The Course *doesn't say it's the only way to get home. But it is certainly suggested that it's a fast way to get home.*

~ **Gary Renard**

"Dreams disappear when light has come and you can see."
-A Course in Miracles

Day 18: Even as one awakens, the dreamland continues. Kenneth Wapnick and I both realized there is no one actually reading these pages, and yet, Ken continued teaching until his apparent death, and I too continue teaching, creating films, books and more. I fully realize I am always teaching myself, reminding myself about the Truth. Today, I invite you to live your life as if you're an actor playing a role. Tonight, share in your journal about the role you played today. -iKE

_____

_____

_____

_____

_____

_____

_____

_____

Teach a class with a *45 Days With* book. Learn how at
www.avaiya.com/45dayswithcourse

The Course *says that the miracle, which is forgiveness, can substitute for learning which may have taken thousands of years. It also says that a miracle, which once again, is forgiveness, can have undreamed of situations and effects of which you are not even aware. It's like "wow," you do these things and a lot of time is being saved by you.*
~ **Gary Renard**

"An unholy relationship is no relationship."
-*A Course in Miracles*

Day 19: Have you witnessed undreamed of situations and effects that you are aware of? Journal today about why or why not. **-Ande**

_____

_____

_____

_____

_____

_____

_____

_____

_____

_____

_____

_____

_____

_____

_____

_____

_____

Teach a class with a *45 Days With* book. Learn how at
www.avaiya.com/45dayswithcourse

The Course *also says that a chief aim of the miracle worker is to save time. What happens as you're doing this kind of forgiveness, is that the Holy Spirit is actually collapsing time. It's possible to change dimensions of time. And all kinds of miraculous things can be happening around you that you're not even aware of because all you see is this little tiny spec of time and space where the Holy Spirit can see everything.*

~ ***Gary Renard***

"It is impossible to overestimate your brother's value."
- A Course in Miracles

Day 20: Today, we invite you to share how much you love everyone. Facebook, Twitter, email, phone calls, etc. Spend part of your day letting everyone here that is part of the Oneness, know you love them. If you're looking to take a Big LEAP!, think of someone you're still holding a grudge against, and let them know you love them. In your journal, share your joy! :-) WE LOVE YOU! -**Ande & iKE**

Teach a class with a *45 Days With* book. Learn how at www.avaiya.com/45dayswithcourse

If you practice forgiveness, you will have the experience that it's working in many different ways. And perhaps the main way that it works is that you feel less upset and more peaceful. Things happen that used to bother you that no longer bother you. And if you're smart and you put two and two together, you start to realize that these things are happening because you've been practicing forgiveness.
~ **Gary Renard**

"Health is the result of relinquishing all attempts to use the body lovelessly." -*A Course in Miracles*

Day 21: Do you feel as healthy as you would like to? Journal about one area in your life that you use the body lovelessly and what you need to forgive to end this separation. Would this bring you a greater experience of peace? I've had the experience of food addictions most of my life, leading me to use my body lovelessly by overeating. The most recent time I revisited this addiction, I forgave it by first being honest about it, and then letting Holy Spirit guide me to eating more moderately. Now journal about your experience. -**Ande**

Teach a class with a *45 Days With* book. Learn how at www.avaiya.com/45dayswithcourse

WEEK 4
Jon Mundy

What forgiveness means in terms of The Course, *is literally that nothing happened. That is, that something only happened in my mind.*

~ Jon Mundy

"Enlightenment is but a recognition, not a change at all."
-A Course in Miracles

Day 22: Most of us know the Albert Einstein quote, "Reality is merely an illusion, albeit a very persistent one." If *The Course* quote above is true, would anything change for you if Enlightenment came knocking at your door? Would there still be a you? For me, nothing changed and everything changed. I still play the character of iKE ALLEN, but my awareness is Oneness. Before Enlightenment, chop wood carry water. After Enlightenment, raise up the thermostat and turn on the faucet. Today, journal about Enlightenment. Not what *The Course* says, what Buddha says, etc. Journal from within yourself and share your thoughts on Enlightenment. **-iKE**

_____

_____

_____

_____

_____

_____

_____

_____

_____

Teach a class with a *45 Days With* book. Learn how at
www.avaiya.com/45dayswithcourse

I'm not saying that something didn't happen in the world. I'm not saying that something didn't happen maybe in a physical way or something like that. But everything is dependent on how I choose to see things.

~ Jon Mundy

"**The Kingdom of Heaven *is* you.**" -*A Course in Miracles*

Day 23: What if you gave up preserving the integrity of your individual self? If The Kingdom of Heaven is you, what would happen? When I sit with the recognition that The Kingdom of Heaven is me, I simultaneously feel great joy, and a twinge of sadness. Open to Holy Spirit today and share in your journal.
-**Ande**

_____

_____

_____

_____

_____

_____

_____

_____

_____

_____

_____

_____

Teach a class with a *45 Days With* book. Learn how at
www.avaiya.com/45dayswithcourse

A very important lesson in A Course in Miracles *is that projection makes perception and you see the world as you make it. Jesus, for example, which is a wonderful example we have, doesn't get upset with the disciples near the end of his life. It doesn't matter that he's going to the cross, because he realizes it doesn't mean anything. They can kill his body, but it's just a body. They can't take away his soul, his spirit, his relationship that he has with God.*

~ **Jon Mundy**

"**You are not the victim of the world you see because you invented it.**" -*A Course in Miracles*

Day 24: I live my life in the knowing that this world came and went long ago and yet, there is still an experience here of an "I" and that "I" has children, friends, clothes, teaches enlightenment seminars, etc. How do you believe your life would occur if you were "Right Minded" all the time? Would there still be a YOU? -iKE

_____
_____
_____
_____
_____
_____
_____
_____
_____
_____
_____

Teach a class with a *45 Days With* book. Learn how at www.avaiya.com/45dayswithcourse

There is really nothing to forgive. But we think that there's something.

***~ Jon Mundy*怀**

"**All things work together for good.**" - *A Course in Miracles*

Day 25: Are you still fighting against forces outside of you? Do you question Jon's words? My words? The *ACIM* quotes? Take a few minutes to focus on what it means to simply be a Mind. Afterwards, share your thoughts in your journal or simply put pen to paper and discover what you write. -i**KE**

Teach a class with a *45 Days With* book. Learn how at www.avaiya.com/45dayswithcourse

If you think about guilt – where does guilt exist? Or, where does unforgiveness exist? It exists in my mind. But it's only in my mind that it exists. Seeing how it exists in my mind, it's also at that level or that point that it can be corrected.
~ Jon Mundy

"**Ask for light and learn that you *are* light.**"
-*A Course in Miracles*

Day 26: What is the biggest challenge of separation in your life today? My biggest challenge is the ego's ever so helpful voice reminding me "If you make a mistake, no one will love you." I acknowledge this voice, saying "Thanks for sharing" and continue following Holy Spirit's guidance to create this book (-: Now, share about your biggest challenge of separation in your journal. -**Ande**

_____

_____

_____

_____

_____

_____

_____

_____

_____

_____

_____

_____

Teach a class with a *45 Days With* book. Learn how at
www.avaiya.com/45dayswithcourse

One of the remarkable things about forgiveness is that when you give it, when you do it – all it really means is "let it go." Just let it go. Alright? The moment you let it go and you say, "it doesn't matter," the miracle is that you then realize, "Oh my God. I'm the one who's forgiven. I'm the one who's liberated. I'm the one who's free."

~ **Jon Mundy**

"The Holy Spirit knows that you both *have* everything and *are* everything." - *A Course in Miracles*

Day 27: Remember, *The Course* is but one theology that leads to God. What if this is a playground for God? What if you are God? How do these questions make you feel today? Do you become angry? Peaceful? Sad? Put pen to paper and discover for yourself.
-iKE

_____

_____

_____

_____

_____

_____

_____

_____

_____

_____

_____

Teach a class with a *45 Days With* book. Learn how at www.avaiya.com/45dayswithcourse

When you practice forgiveness and let go, you realize, "This was weighing on me. This was heavy on me - this thing I couldn't let go of." It could be a really big thing or it could be a small thing. It doesn't make a difference what it is. It's still exactly the same process of letting go and the result is peace.
~ **Jon Mundy**

"Everything outside the Kingdom is illusion."
- A Course in Miracles

Day 28: Think for a moment about a small thing you're holding onto and then, let it go. I've been holding onto a grievance toward my friend, who showed up late to our lunch meeting recently. Now, I let it go! Often, it is the small things that weigh us down. **-Ande**

Teach a class with a *45 Days With* book. Learn how at
www.avaiya.com/45dayswithcourse

WEEK 5
Nouk Sanchez

You and this entire room are all coming from one source as far as I'm concerned. And that is my own projection. So anything that may push my buttons in my life is coming from me. It's my projection. It's coming from the separated self, the small me, the small mind, the Ego. Whenever my buttons are pressed, it's a perfect opportunity for forgiveness.
~ **Nouk Sanchez**

"The world you see does not exist." -*A Course in Miracles*

Day 29: When you consider it's all truly coming from you, what emotions do you feel? Today, journal about the emotions you're feeling while considering this. Do not think, simply put pen to paper and let the words flow, much like Helen did when she scribed *The Course*. **-iKE & Ande**

_____

_____

_____

_____

_____

_____

_____

_____

_____

_____

_____

_____

Teach a class with a *45 Days With* book. Learn how at www.avaiya.com/45dayswithcourse

Whenever my buttons are pressed, I can then go, "Okay. It's not about me going outside of myself and changing you if you press my buttons, or changing this room if it doesn't suit me." Because that's just a distraction from what's really happening. It's just the effect of what's happening. What I need to do is recognize that the cause comes from within me. And it's about just saying, "Okay. How am I feeling? What's happening for me right now? What is causing this?"

~ **Nouk Sanchez**

"The world you see has nothing to do with reality."
-A Course in Miracles

Day 30: Where are you in your journey today? Are you feeling fearful or anxious? Are you experiencing love and peace? As I write this action step, I'm watching a beautiful sunrise in Colorado and looking at pictures of my two daughters with a large grin on my face. Share your feelings again today. Put your pen on the journal page below and witness what appears on the paper as you open up to Holy Spirit. -iKE

_____

_____

_____

_____

_____

_____

_____

_____

_____

Teach a class with a *45 Days With* book. Learn how at
www.avaiya.com/45dayswithcourse

When I forgive everything that seems to be pressing my buttons outside, including you or forgiving the circumstances around me that I can't do anything about, my undoing - the undoing of the idea of separation which is the Ego - begins to occur. Then it's like a rolling stone. It just unfolds and unfolds, so the only thing that we really need to do, in my belief is that every time life presses our buttons, don't avoid it. Don't resist it. Resistance is just perpetuating the dream. Let's embrace it. See it as an opportunity for forgiveness. It's an opportunity for us to look and remember that the source of this is here.
*~ **Nouk Sanchez***

"Your goal is to find out who you are."
-A Course in Miracles

Day 31: Do you believe you truly want to awaken? Are you willing to remove *all* the blocks to love's presence? Today, journal about why you want the direct experience of Truth. Do you feel Holy Spirit helping you write in your journal today? -iKE

Forgiveness is not about secretly judging ourselves, which is where I got lost on the spiritual journey for many, many years. I would withdraw my projections from the outside world and from others, but secretly judge myself while at the same time thinking I was free. My life seemed to be getting a lot more joyous, a lot more peaceful. But, then I found that "ah-ha." The Ego is a tricky little bastard. It really is sneaky.
~ **Nouk Sanchez**

"Can you imagine what a state of mind without illusions is?" -*A Course in Miracles*

Day 32: Where are you secretly judging yourself? I am judging myself for not being as in shape, physically, as I was 5 years ago. Place your pen on the page and share. -**Ande**

_____

_____

_____

_____

_____

_____

_____

_____

_____

_____

_____

_____

_____

Teach a class with a *45 Days With* book. Learn how at www.avaiya.com/45dayswithcourse

The ego is often just taking the judgment from outside and turning it inside. Now most people would say, "Oh, well, it's not so bad if you're self-judging."
~ **Nouk Sanchez**

"**To mean you want the peace of God is to renounce all dreams.**" -*A Course in Miracles*

Day 33: Today, ask Holy Spirit for guidance in letting go of self-judging. Put pen to paper and allow Holy Spirit to show you the way. -**Ande**

As you evolve on your spiritual journey, you realize, "Wow. There's no hierarchy of illusions with this Ego." Judging another, judging the situation or a thing, and judging yourself - they're both the same. So here I was thinking that I was undoing all of these Ego projections only to find, "Hey. The Ego's judging itself." I'm sure that a lot of people on a spiritual journey can identify with this. Now on my spiritual journey, I am working on how to undo the self-judgment. And, it's working.
~ **Nouk Sanchez**

"Heaven itself is reached with empty hands and open minds." -*A Course in Miracles*

Day 34: For me, freedom from illusions is maintained by accepting "What Is," and not judging it, as judgment only leads to guilt. Today, place your pen on the page and imagine one illusion of guilt you could let go of today. Scribe or journal about this today. -iKE

_____

_____

_____

_____

_____

_____

_____

_____

_____

_____

_____

_____

_____

Teach a class with a *45 Days With* book. Learn how at www.avaiya.com/45dayswithcourse

The only thing we need to do is withdraw our judgment from the world that seems to be outside of us and to look at anything we resist. If there is a circumstance that we can't change, we need to accept it. And then gradually replace that with gratitude for anything that might press our buttons and allow us to practice forgiveness.

~ ***Nouk Sanchez***

"There is a place in you where there is perfect peace."
-*A Course in Miracles*

Day 35: Today, journal about one circumstance you cannot change in your life, but you're still trying to. Share your thoughts on what it would take to let go. For me, something I want to change but cannot, is my mother having breast cancer. In my process of letting this go, I'm constantly reminding myself that a perfect outcome is assured. **-Ande**

Teach a class with a *45 Days With* book. Learn how at www.avaiya.com/45dayswithcourse

WEEK 6
Linda Carpenter

There is really only one place where we can find a state of peace, an experience of love. And that comes from within the mind that is more aligned with that God self. We begin our experience in physicality looking for it outside ourselves in this world. And many people never go beyond that point and are always disappointed because in this world, there is constant change. There are constant opposites. So there is not a state of peace, of lasting peace in this state of the world.

~ **Linda Carpenter**

45 Days with *A Course in Miracles*

"The first step toward freedom involves a sorting out of the false from the true." -*A Course in Miracles*

Day 36: One seeming paradox is, it's not happening, but you have the experience of it happening. My experience is that the storyline of life appears to keep moving while my awareness continuously knows nothing is here. My life is much like a play. I say my lines as an actor and have no interest in rewriting them along the way. I enjoy the show as it rolls out. Do you truly want to be free? Are you willing to let go of your beliefs about reality? Your beliefs about this book? Share or scribe authentically in your journal today.
-iKE

_____

_____

_____

_____

_____

_____

_____

_____

_____

Teach a class with a *45 Days With* book. Learn how at
www.avaiya.com/45dayswithcourse

One of the great teachings of The Course *is the understanding of the difference between cause and effect. That the world is not the cause of our experiences. It is our state of mind and how we believe we see ourselves. And, of course, if we come into physicality, we bring with us the feeling that we are separate. We bring in with us the feeling that we are going to find struggle and suffering and certainly death. And, underlying it all is the feeling that there is something wrong with us, which then is portrayed outside in the world. From that state of mind, peace can never be found.~* **Linda Carpenter**

"To learn this course requires willingness to question every value that you hold." - *A Course in Miracles*

Day 37: Imagine how enjoyable life would be if you simply watched it unfold. Today, share or scribe in your journal about a life of surrendering into a world that came and went a long time ago. When I am challenged in life, reminding myself that everything appearing to happen is perfect, because it already happened, brings me great peace. **-Ande**

Teach a class with a *45 Days With* book. Learn how at www.avaiya.com/45dayswithcourse

A lasting change of thought can never be found in judgment. Because it's not the nature of the world or the mind that created it, to have that experience.

~ *Linda Carpenter*

"The Holy Spirit's Voice is as loud as your willingness to listen." - *A Course in Miracles*

Day 38: How many times in your life have you felt nudged to not judge, but ignored the nudge? Today, sit quietly for a few minutes and once you feel nudged by Holy Spirit to write about something, regardless of what it is, put pen to paper and share it in your journal. -iKE

_____

_____

_____

_____

_____

_____

_____

_____

_____

_____

_____

_____

_____

Teach a class with a *45 Days With* book. Learn how at www.avaiya.com/45dayswithcourse

When we move within our minds, we learn that the voice of God, what we call the Holy Spirit, holds the awareness of peace for us. It is like that beautiful phrase in the Bible, "The peace that passes understanding."

~ ***Linda Carpenter***

"**Love is freedom.**" -*A Course in Miracles*

Day 39: Where in your life are you feeling peaceful and free today? I am experiencing great peace and freedom today, as I feel the loving presence of Holy Spirit surround me. Share about your experience in your journal. -**Ande**

_____

_____

_____

_____

_____

_____

_____

_____

_____

_____

_____

_____

Teach a class with a *45 Days With* book. Learn how at www.avaiya.com/45dayswithcourse

There is nothing in this world that can justify the peace of God.

~ Linda Carpenter

"There is no substitute for peace." - *A Course in Miracles*

Day 40: Make a miracle filled with peace happen! Give it every ounce of your love. Journal about it and fill your page with agape. **-iKE**

Teach a class with a *45 Days With* book. Learn how at www.avaiya.com/45dayswithcourse

As we begin to trust that peace of mind - the stability and deep comfort of that peace of mind - then we begin to experience more peace in our daily life, while we're still in this physical experience that seems to be very tempted to find disempowering experiences.

*~ **Linda Carpenter***

"Forgiveness is the end of specialness."
-A Course in Miracles

Day 41: Are you ready to bathe in peace and ignore the voice of the ego? In my *Awakening To Authenticity* coaching program, I guide people to confront the very core of the egoic manufacturing facility and let that thought system know it's chatter is no longer of interest to them. Today put pen to paper and write a lovingly appreciative letter to the ego, letting it know that although the chatter will always be present, you will no longer be listening to it. -iKE

Teach a class with a *45 Days With* book. Learn how at www.avaiya.com/45dayswithcourse

I think for most of us who follow The Course *or other teachings of non-duality, we find that the inner peace grows and becomes deeper, the love becomes more all-encompassing and this brings great joy into our lives.*

~ **Linda Carpenter**

"You must choose between total freedom and total bondage." -*A Course in Miracles*

Day 42: Do you believe in peace? Can you do something today to live and demonstrate forgiveness? Afterwards, journal about what happened. Today, I live and demonstrate forgiveness by being aware each time the ego says something self-deprecating, and then letting it go. -**Ande**

_____

_____

_____

_____

_____

_____

_____

_____

_____

_____

_____

_____

Teach a class with a *45 Days With* book. Learn how at www.avaiya.com/45dayswithcourse

WEEK 7
Kenneth Wapnick

The benefit of forgiveness is that we will feel better – pure and simple. Not that necessarily my body would feel better, not that my bank account would feel better, not that my children would no longer be sick, not that things would change in the world, but I'll have Peace of Mind.

~ Kenneth Wapnick

"Reality can dawn only on an unclouded mind."
-A Course in Miracles

Day 43: When I first met Ken in Temecula, California we had a playfully fun conversation in his office while we were alone. He looked at me and said, "Oh, you're like me." I coyly replied with, "Yes, but I have more hair." We then talked about what it was like to live in a world of sleeping giants and how seldom we each ran into other awakened people. We shared with each other about how we both felt compelled to help awaken others, not because there was actually anyone out there, but simply because it was our most natural expression. Spending time with Ken was like looking in a mirror. We both possessed the ongoing awareness of the Truth of who and what we really were. We both understood we were the same thing, having separate experiences. The conversation ended with Ken saying, "Okay, let's go back out there and play our roles." Ken and I had a wonderful experience where we both knew we were One. Today, journal about a moment in your life when you and another blended together into oneness. -iKE

_____

_____

_____

_____

_____

_____

_____

_____

Teach a class with a *45 Days With* book. Learn how at
www.avaiya.com/45dayswithcourse

The Source of all of our discomfort is a projection of our guilt. That's why we're so uncomfortable. There's a line in The Course *that says, "Of all the many causes of your suffering, you never thought your guilt was among them." Actually, to be even more precise, the cause of our suffering is not guilt, because how can what's non-existent be the cause of suffering? The cause of our suffering is our Mind's belief in guilt. That's the problem. Separation from God can't be the problem. Guilt can't be the problem. The world can't be the problem. What doesn't exist can't be the problem. The problem is that our deluded Mind has believed the lies of the Ego. And it's our Mind's decision for the Ego, and therefore for guilt, that's the problem. So what forgiveness does, is gently erase all that.*
~ **Kenneth Wapnick**

"There is no road to travel on, and no time to travel through." -*A Course in Miracles*

Day 44: Ken clearly reminds us of our guilt and the lies of the ego. Where can you let go today? I can let go of the ego's lie that "I have to prove to people that I'm loveable for them to love me." Share or scribe in your journal today. -**Ande**

_____

_____

_____

_____

_____

_____

_____

_____

_____

_____

_____

Teach a class with a *45 Days With* book. Learn how at www.avaiya.com/45dayswithcourse

What is left when guilt is gone, is the Love and the Peace of God, because the guilt was literally made to cover that over. And from that Love and that Peace, no matter what goes on in the world around us, we would retain that Peace and that quiet Joy.
~ **Kenneth Wapnick**

"The special love relationship is an attempt to bring love into separation." -*A Course in Miracles*

Day 45: Today, simply make a list of every past romantic relationship and every friendship you have ever had that ended badly. That's it! For me, I realized, I'm not friends with any of my ex-boyfriends. Hmmm...there's something for me to write about today (-: -**Ande**

_____
_____
_____
_____
_____
_____
_____
_____
_____
_____

Teach a class with a *45 Days With* book. Learn how at www.avaiya.com/45dayswithcourse

BONUS DAYS!

The beginning of Lesson 155 says, "You will smile more frequently and your forehead will be serene." In other words, you'll be peaceful. And it doesn't mean that you'll walk around all day literally with a smile on your face, but the inner smile is not giving anything in the world power over you.
~ **Kenneth Wapnick**

"The world you see is the delusional system of those made mad by guilt." -*A Course in Miracles*

Day 46: Today, look at the list you made yesterday. Next to each person's name, honestly list whose fault you currently think it was that the relationship ended - yours or theirs. -iKE

You don't deny there's a world out there, you don't deny what goes on in the world, but you deny – in the Right-Minded sense of deny – you deny the power of anything outside of you to affect this sweet smile within you and this quiet joy. That's what forgiveness offers and that's what forgiveness promises, and that's the goal of this Course.
~ **Kenneth Wapnick**

"Love and guilt cannot coexist, and to accept one is to deny the other." -*A Course in Miracles*

Day 47: If noBODY else is a sinner, are you? If noBODY else is even here, are you? Perhaps you are still safely at home? We believe you are. Have a wonderFULL day. -**Ande & iKE**

Teach a class with a *45 Days With* book. Learn how at www.avaiya.com/45dayswithcourse

There's a wonderful line saying that when you cross over to the real world, which is **The Course's** *symbol for the end of the journey, you will realize "in glad astonishment that for all this, you gave up nothing." But on this side of the bridge, we're giving up everything. We're giving up not only what we cherish and what we love, but we're giving up our very self.*
~ **Kenneth Wapnick**

"Forget this world, forget this course...."
-*A Course in Miracles*

Day 48: Walt Whitman said, "Do I contradict myself? Very well, then I contradict myself, I am large, I contain multitudes." Often, life appears to be a contradiction. We are here, we are not here. We should study this Course, we should forget this Course. What is a big contradiction in your life right now? Share it in your journal today.
-iKE

_____
_____
_____
_____
_____
_____
_____
_____
_____
_____

Teach a class with a *45 Days With* book. Learn how at
www.avaiya.com/45dayswithcourse

When I forgive, it's when I basically fire the Ego as my teacher saying, "I no longer want to learn from you." I now choose a different teacher, the Holy Spirit or Jesus – that's my holy relationship.
~ **Kenneth Wapnick**

"Guilt feelings are the preservers of time."
-A Course in Miracles

Day 49: Today is a great day to reflect on all the love you've experienced on this journey. Make a list of what you feel is left to confront and then, celebrate this amazing journey we've had together! -**Ande & iKE**

In addition, congratulate yourSELF as this is your final day. We hope you have had a joyful journey with *A Course in Miracles* and US. Here is a wonderFULL final insight from Kenneth Wapnick:

"If you really knew and believed the world were an illusion, you would not see anyone as separate. Because what "the world is an illusion" means is that God's reality of perfect Oneness is the Truth, which means everyone here is part of that Oneness. When you are totally Right-Minded - which really comes from that understanding and appreciation that the world is an illusion and the only reality is the Non-Dual reality, there's only Spirit and Truth and nothing else - then everything you do will come from that place of Truth in your Mind and it will be totally loving and will not exclude anyone, but embrace everyone."
~ **Kenneth Wapnick**

Ken passed away on December 27, 2013.

You can additionally see Ken and other *ACIM* teachers featured in our books, films and more, available at www.avaiya.com/ACIM.

ABOUT THE AUTHORS

iKE ALLEN and **Ande Anderson**, MS, RD, are international speakers, seminar leaders and the founders of AVAIYA (www.AVAIYA.com). AVAIYA creates positive media such as the book series, *45 Days With*, including *45 Days with Kenneth Wapnick*, & the films *A Course in Miracles The Movie*, the ACIM-inspired musical documentary, *Reverend Yolanda's Old Time Gospel Hour The Movie*, the upcoming title, *Remembering Kenneth Wapnick,* and the *A Course in Miracles Awakening Series* video and audio courses. iKE & Ande are the creators of the interactive video presentation, *Unity in A Course in Miracles*, featuring rare video footage of Kenneth Wapnick, Gary Renard, Jon Mundy, David Hoffmeister and more. They live in Boulder, Colorado. For speaking engagements, seminars and more, visit www.AVAIYA.com.

Teach a class with a *45 Days With* book. Learn how at
www.avaiya.com/45dayswithcourse

AVAIYA
NEW THOUGHT NETWORK

AVAIYA
experience conscious living
A Colorado Company

Would you like to have AVAIYA filmmakers iKE ALLEN & Ande Anderson visit your center and show one of their films?

Our films feature Visionaries like:

- Gay Hendricks
- Janet Attwood
- Marci Shimoff
- Fred Alan Wolf
- Judith Orloff
- Joan Borysenko
- Joe Dispenza
- Amit Goswami
- James Twyman
- Cynthia James
- Gary Renard
- Mary Morrissey
- Mike Dooley
- and many others

iKE & Dan Millman
Bob Proctor & Ande
Us with Mary Morrissey
Us with Mike Dooley
Ande & Alan Cohen
iKE & Joe Vitale

Learn more about how iKE & Ande can come to your business, church or center to show one of their powerful films on Perception, Gratitude, Diversity, etc. and lead a discussion following the film with Q&A.

www.AVAIYA.com

45 Days with *A Course in Miracles*

NOTES

Teach a class with a *45 Days With* book. Learn how at www.avaiya.com/45dayswithcourse

NOTES

NOTES

Teach a class with a *45 Days With* book. Learn how at
www.avaiya.com/45dayswithcourse

NOTES

NOTES

Teach a class with a *45 Days With* book. Learn how at www.avaiya.com/45dayswithcourse

NOTES

NOTES

Teach a class with a *45 Days With* book. Learn how at
www.avaiya.com/45dayswithcourse

NOTES

Made in the USA
Las Vegas, NV
01 August 2021